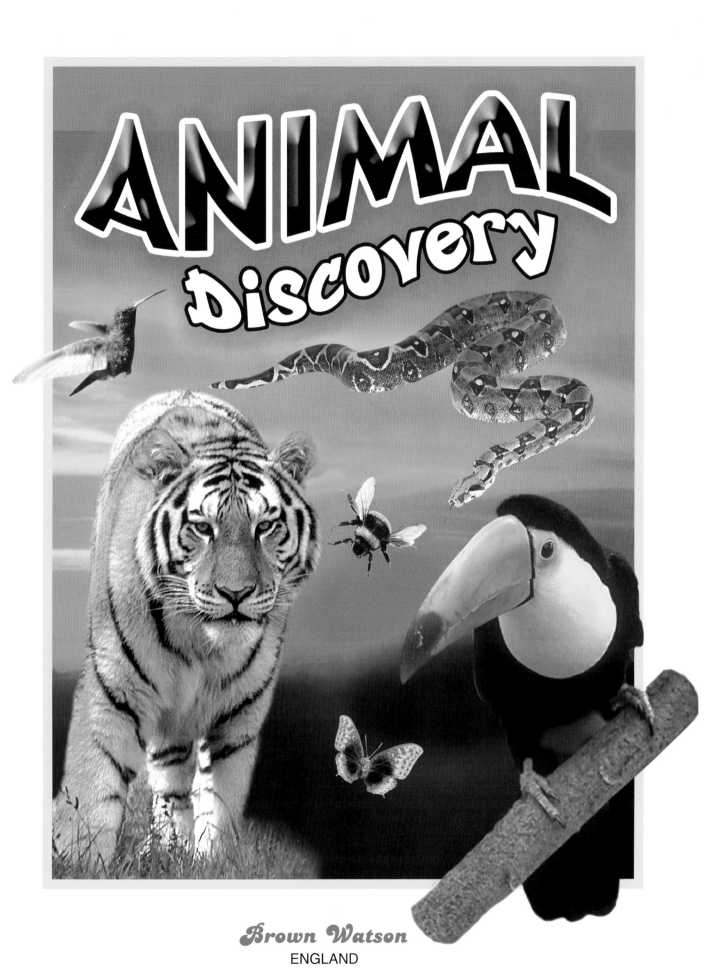

ANIMAL
Discovery

Brown Watson
ENGLAND

This edition first published 2006 by
Brown Watson, The Old Mill
76 Fleckney Road
Kibworth Beauchamp
Leicestershire LE8 0HG

ISBN: 978-0-7097-1754-6
Reprinted 2007

CONTENTS

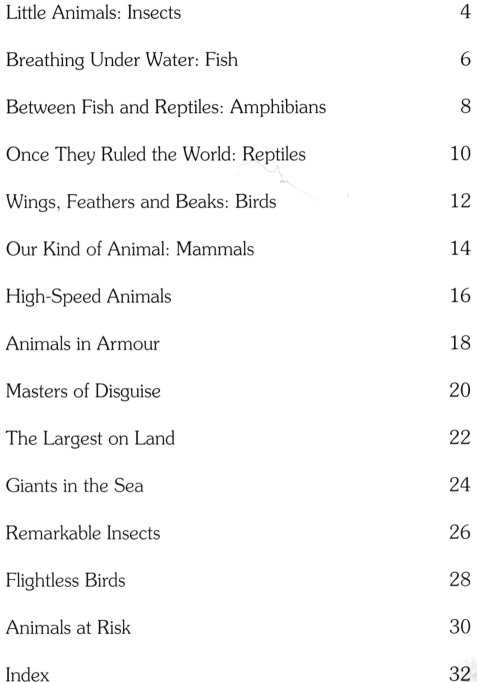

LITTLE ANIMALS: INSECTS

Around a million different kinds of insects have been discovered so far, making them the largest and most varied form of animal life. There could be another 30 million varieties to be discovered! Insects are small creatures, with bodies divided into three parts, each part with a pair of legs. They live everywhere, though there are very few in the sea.

LOCUST

Length: 5–7cm

The locust is the largest of the grasshoppers. The Migratory Locust is a fearsome pest in many places, destroying crops and natural vegetation. So many swarm together and migrate that the sky becomes dark. About 120 years ago in America, a swarm of Rocky Mountain Locusts (a species that has since died out) was estimated as covering over 250,000 sq km, and took five days to pass over someone on the ground!

TERMITE

Length: 2cm

Like ants, termites live in large, underground colonies, or tall, mud towers, so strong that it has taken explosives to destroy them! One term mound was found to be nearly 9m high! Sometimes called 'white ants', termites are actually more closely related to cockroaches. When one termite species marches through the African forest, the sound of millions c their heads striking the ground can be heard from many kilometres away.

4

BEETLE
Length: 0.5mm–19cm

With about 250,000 different species, beetles are the largest group of insects. All have biting mouths, and tough, horny, front wings, which cover and protect the delicate rear wings that are used for flying. The Hercules Beetle shown here is one of the largest, though its horn accounts for more than half its length.

HONEY BEE
Length: 1.2–1.8cm

Like all bees, Honey Bees have stocky, hairy bodies. They are social insects, with up to 50,000 living together in a colony. In the wild, they build their wax nests in hollow trees. Man-made beehives are accepted as just another kind of hollow tree! It is the worker bees who fly from flower to flower, collecting pollen (on their body hairs) and eating nectar (from which honey is made). In flight, their wings move up and down more than 200 times a second, and they may travel over 90km in a day.

DRAGONFLY
Wingspan: 10.6cm

Like other dragonflies, the Emperor Dragonfly flies very fast. Its eyes cover most of its head, enabling it to spot and catch other insects in flight. Dragonfly eggs are scattered into water or laid on underwater plants. From an egg, a nymph (an insect in the feeding and growth stages of development) is hatched. When ready, it climbs up a plant out of the water, where its skin splits open and the young dragonfly emerges.

BREATHING UNDER WATER: FISH

Fish are cold-blooded animals with backbones that live all their lives in water, breathing oxygen from it through their gills. There are over 20,000 species of fish, most living in saltwater. About a third live in freshwater. As you can see from the examples shown here, fish come in all shapes and sizes.

ELECTRIC EEL

Length: up to 2.4m

This large freshwater fish lives in South America, in the Amazon and Orinoco Rivers. It generates an electric shock of over 500 volts, strong enough to disable a man. It uses this power to kill its prey, and as a defence. Since it lives in very dark waters, the Electric Eel also 'bounces' electrical pulses off its surroundings as an aid to navigation.

FLATFISH

Length: 120mm–2.4m

We eat many kinds of flatfish, like Halibut, Sole, and Plaice. When they hatch from eggs, flatfish have an eye each side of their mouths. As they grow, one side of the body becomes coloured to match the sea bottom where they feed, and one eye moves round to join the other on the coloured side. The 'blind side' remains colourless. Strangely, each flatfish species consistently has eyes to one particular side of the mouth. Turbots' eyes are always to the right; halibuts' the left.

SEAHORSE

Length: up to 30cm

The seahorse is a 'tube-mouth' fish, meaning it has a long, tube-like snout, which gives it its unique, horse-like head. It swims upright in the water. For about five weeks after the female has laid her eggs, they are carried by the male seahorse in a special pouch, until they hatch out as miniature versions of the adults.

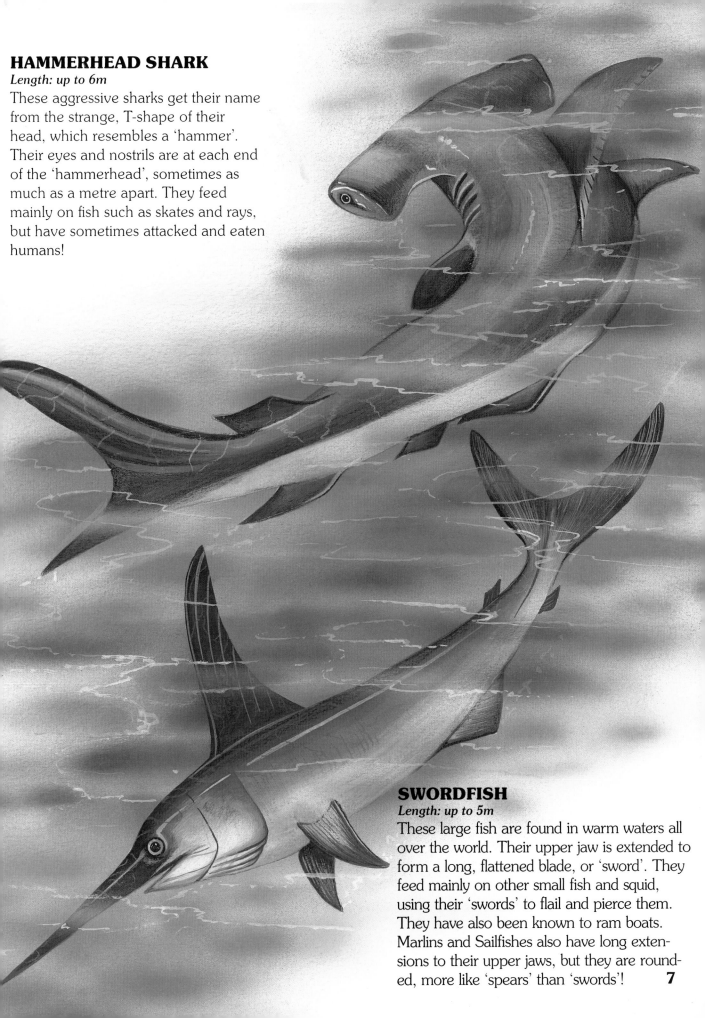

HAMMERHEAD SHARK
Length: up to 6m

These aggressive sharks get their name from the strange, T-shape of their head, which resembles a 'hammer'. Their eyes and nostrils are at each end of the 'hammerhead', sometimes as much as a metre apart. They feed mainly on fish such as skates and rays, but have sometimes attacked and eaten humans!

SWORDFISH
Length: up to 5m

These large fish are found in warm waters all over the world. Their upper jaw is extended to form a long, flattened blade, or 'sword'. They feed mainly on other small fish and squid, using their 'swords' to flail and pierce them. They have also been known to ram boats. Marlins and Sailfishes also have long extensions to their upper jaws, but they are rounded, more like 'spears' than 'swords'!

BETWEEN FISH AND REPTILES: AMPHIBIANS

The cold-blooded amphibians are really halfway between fish and reptiles. Most spend the first part of their lives in water, moving onto land as they become adults. They are found close to freshwater, or in wet places, but no amphibians live in the sea. There are about 4,000 different species in the world.

FROG

Length: 12mm–36.8cm

To scientists, both frogs and toads are classified within the same group of amphibians without tails. The only difference is that frogs have smooth, wet skin, while toads have rough, dry skin. Frogs are found everywhere in the world, except the Arctic and Antarctic. The strongest known poison comes from the skin of the Golden Poison-Dart Frog in South America. One frog has enough poison to kill 1,500 people!

TOAD

Length: under 24mm–over 24cm

Toads are able to exist at higher altitudes than frogs. One has even been found in the Himalayas at a height of 8,000 metres. It can also be dangerous to touch their skin, because they can give off a whitish fluid which can cause severe burning to a person's eyes or mouth. As with frogs, they lay their eggs in water, where they hatch into tadpoles, which later move onto land to become adult toads.

SALAMANDER and NEWT
Length: under 15mm – 1.8m

Salamanders and newts are amphibians with tails. Salamanders look like lizards, which are reptiles, but salamanders have no claws, nor scales on their bodies. Most are active only at night, avoiding direct light. Some species, like the Olm, in Europe, live in underground streams and caves, and are completely blind. If a salamander loses a leg or its tail, it can grow a new one! Newts are familiar sights in garden ponds. Some are brightly coloured and have a crest running down their back.

CAECILIAN
pronounced 'SEE-sill-yan'
Length: 10cm – 1.4m

The Caecilians are blind amphibians *without legs*! They look rather like worms with jaws and teeth. They live in swamps or in streams in tropical parts of the world, but since they are very difficult to find even when you are looking for them, you probably will never see one in the wild!

9

ONCE THEY RULED THE WORLD: REPTILES

Reptiles evolved from amphibians. For a long period of 160 million years in earth's history, reptiles were the dominant form of life on the planet, and existed in an enormous variety of shapes and sizes. We still do not really understand why their reign ended about 65 million years ago. Shown here are some of the reptiles in our world today.

CROCODILE and ALLIGATOR
Length: from 1m–7m

The crocodile family includes alligators, caymans, and gavials, and is descended almost unchanged in 65 million years from its dinosaur ancestors. To tell a crocodile from an alligator, look at them when the jaws are closed. If the fourth tooth from the front is sticking out, it's a crocodile! All have rough skins, long, strong tails, and are superb swimmers. The Nile Crocodile lives in the great River Nile in Africa. It often sleeps in the sun with its mouth open, while birds called plovers hop in and out, cleaning its teeth! Herodotus, a Greek historian and voyager, first mentioned this in his writings 2,500 years ago!

LIZARD
Length: 18mm–3.1m

Except in very cold areas, lizards live all over the world, ranging in size from tiny Geckos in Central America to the dragon-like Komodo Monitors in Indonesia. The Australian Thorny Devil is protected by the sharp spines on its back, and the South American Basilisk Lizard can actually run across water for several metres on its back legs! The Draco of South-East Asia 'flies', or glides, from tree to tree, thanks to flaps along its sides. All lizards have cold blood, and dry, scaly, watertight skin.

SNAKE
Length: 10cm–10m

There are about 2,500 different species of snake, and 300 have poisonous bites, though only about 50 are dangerous to man, causing around 40,000 deaths each year. Sea snakes are much more venomous than those on land. Snakes have no ears, but 'hear' through sensing vibrations on the ground. Their jaws are not hinged like ours, but can open wide enough to swallow something that is many times larger than their own head! The heaviest snake of all is the Anaconda, which can weigh over 225kg.

11

WINGS, FEATHERS AND BEAKS: BIRDS

Only birds have feathers, and all adult birds have feathers, even if they cannot fly! Feathers are light, and the bones of most birds are hollow, which keeps their weight down, making it easier for them to get off the ground. Out of around 8,600 species of birds, most are small. They are present all over the world, except at the poles or in the deep sea. Birds lay eggs, and have warm blood. Without the sounds of birds, our world would be a much poorer place.

NIGHTINGALE

Length: about 16.5cm

The Thrush family contains some of the world's most beloved songbirds, like the blackbird, the robin, the songthrush…and the nightingale. Nightingales pass the winter in Africa, returning to Europe for the spring and summer. Only the male bird sings, but, in the spring, when singing to attract a female, the nightingale's song is unforgettable, and much loved by poets!

SWAN

Length: up to 1.5m

The long-necked swans are waterfowl, the largest and most gracious, but in the same family as geese and ducks.

There are 10 species. Best-known is the Mute Swan, so often seen on our rivers and ponds. It is not really mute, since it can make hissing noises, but it is very bad-tempered, so you are advised not to go too close! Mute Swans were domesticated in England more than 800 years ago.

BIRDS OF PARADISE
Length: up to 46cm

When the only ship to survive the first round-the-world voyage returned to Spain in 1522, it brought back two bird of paradise skins. The Spaniards were sure that such a beautiful bird could only live in paradise! Today, there are 43 species, all living in South-East Asia. It is only the male bird that has the gorgeous display of plumage, to attract females.

EAGLE
Length: up to 1m

Eagles, with their hooked beaks, are great birds of prey. The Golden Eagle was a symbol of the power of Ancient Rome, and an image of the bird was carried on a staff before each legion in the Roman army. The Bald Eagle, the national bird of the United States, eats fish. If it cannot catch its own, it steals from other birds! It is not really bald. Its head and neck are covered in white feathers. Its nests are the biggest of all bird's-nests, measuring as much as 6 metres wide by nearly 3 metres deep!

OUR KIND OF ANIMAL: MAMMALS

Mammals are warm-blooded animals, with bodies completely, or partly, covered in hair. Their newborn young are fed on their mothers' milk. Mammals are widespread on land. Bats are flying mammals. Whales, dolphins, and porpoises are marine mammals. Man is a mammal, and his closest relatives are monkeys, which have tails, and apes, like gorillas and chimpanzees, which are tail-less.

CHIMPANZEE

Height: up to 1.3m

Of all the apes, the chimpanzee most resembles us. Its body is covered in hair, though its face is not. Chimpanzees live in the forests of central Africa, travelling in groups of to 20 individuals, with a male leader. They are unusual animals, since they can use tools, employing twigs for fishing and stones as hammers. Sadly because they are so intelligent and like us, we use many chimpanzees for experiments in our laboratories.

LION

Weight: up to 313kg

Lions are members of the cat family, the only cats to live and hunt in groups, called 'prides'. A pride of lions consists of related females and young, with one or two adult males. Generally, it is the lionesses who do the hunting, but after the prey is killed, the lions eat first, followed by the lionesses, with the cubs feeding last of all! They are carnivores, or flesh-eaters. Nowadays, they survive in the wild only in East Africa, and in one small part of India.

SEAL
Weight: up to 4,000kg

The 19 species of seals are carnivorous mammals that live in water. All are furry, with a thick layer of fat, called blubber, beneath the skin. The Grey seal is a common sight off the coasts of Europe and North America. Weddell seals live in the bitter Antarctic Ocean, where the sea freezes over. In order to breathe, they have to chew holes in the ice! The largest seal is the Elephant seal, growing to over 6.5 metres in length. It gets its name from the 30cm-long 'trunk' on the male's head, which it inflates when it is excited.

DUCK-BILLED PLATYPUS
Length: up to 75cm

This is one of the most primitive mammals. Its fur-covered head, body and tail are flattened. Its eyes, like a reptile, are on the sides of its head, it has webbed feet, and a duck-like beak. And it lays eggs! After its young hatch out, they lick milk from the fur on their mother's stomach. The platypus lives in the rivers of Australia and Tasmania. It sleeps by day in burrows which can be over 30 metres deep, and hunts worms and shrimps by night.

HIGH-SPEED ANIMALS

The fastest human athletes can reach speeds of just over 43 kilometres per hour. The fastest land animal can more than double that! The fastest bird can fly more than seven times faster! Shown here are four high-speed animals.

PEREGRINE FALCON
Length: about 45cm

This bird of prey can be found all over the world, though its numbers are declining because the widespread use of pesticides is affecting the hatching of its eggs. Peregrine falcons hunt from high in the air, swooping down on other birds at tremendous speeds. A diving peregrine is the fastest living creature, and can reach speeds of 350 kilometres an hour. The falcon strikes its prey cleanly with its talons, killing it instantly.

CHEETAH
Weight: up to 65kg

Though it is actually a big cat, the cheetah, or hunting leopard, has much in common with dogs! It does not climb, it has long legs, and it hunts by running down its prey, rather than stalking and pouncing on it, as other cats do. When chasing antelopes, the cheetah can achieve speeds of over 100 kilometres an hour, but only for a few hundred metres. It survives now only in some parts of Africa.

HUMMINGBIRD
Length: 6.0–21.6mm

The hummingbirds of North and South America are the most colourful of all birds, tiny jewels who depend for their food entirely on flowers. They are also the supreme fliers of the bird world, able just as easily to dart about, stop suddenly, hang in the air, and even fly backwards! Though they are not the world's speediest fliers, their wings beat so quickly, up to 90 times a second, that they are just a blur to our eyes. It is the humming noise of their wings which gives these birds their name.

PRONGHORN ANTELOPE
Weight: up to 65kg

Over longer distances than the cheetah, the pronghorn antelope can run at over 88 kilometres per hour. Once these small animals lived in great herds all over western North America, but most were killed in the last century by white hunters. The pronghorn antelope gets its name from the fact that it is the only member of the antelope family with divided, or pronged, horns.

ANIMALS IN ARMOUR

Animals have different ways of keeping out of trouble. Some can run very fast away from it. Some are so well camouflaged that they are difficult to find. Some take refuge up in trees, or vanish into holes in the ground. And there are a few animals who don't have to worry much about any trouble! They live inside their own armour-plating!

TORTOISE and TURTLE

Weight: Tortoise up to 298kg: Turtle 960kg

Tortoises and turtles belong to the same family. Species living on land are called tortoises: those living in fresh or seawater are called turtles. They are the oldest type of living reptiles, having been on earth for over 170 million years, with very little change in some cases! Most have hard shells, into which they can pull their head, legs, and tail, for protection. All lay their eggs in sand, leaving them to be hatched out by the sun's heat. Their toothless jaws form a hard beak, and they live to a great age, over 150 years in one instance!

18

RMADILLO
eight: 90g–55kg

ny animal that hopes to make a meal
f an armadillo has problems, for the
rmadillo's back, head, sides, and tail
re covered in bony armour! In
ddition, when attacked, some
rmadillos roll into a tight ball, while
thers dig quickly out of sight in the
round. Most armadillos live in South
merica, a few as far north as the
outhern United States. They live in
roups in burrows, and are mainly
sect-eaters, with lots of tiny teeth.
iant Armadillos have almost 100
eth, more than any other mammal.

RHINOCEROS
Weight: up to 3,900kg

The only land animal larger than the rhinoceros is the
elephant. A rhino can be over 2m high, and nearly
5m long! Its thick, folded skin is as tough as armour-
plating, and depending on its species, it will have one
or two horns on its nose. When angered, rhinos can
charge at up to 40km/h, and there is a record of one
derailing a train! Yet this strange-looking, short-sighted
animal is actually a shy vegetarian! Most rhinos lead
solitary lives; they bathe a lot, and can swim well.

MASTERS OF DISGUISE

The skins or coats of many animals are coloured in ways that make them difficult to see. This 'disguise' helps them to blend into the background, so that they can hide from hunters. And, if they are hunters themselves, a good disguise gives them more chance of catching their next meal! Some animals change their skin colour according to what they happen to be standing on at the time! Some, for survival, 'copy' the appearance of another creature.

TIGER

Weight: up to 423kg

Tigers are the largest members of the cat family. Once, they ranged widely over Asia, but now there are probably only about 3,000 tigers living in the wild. They are spectacular to look at, and graceful in their movements. They keep to the dark forests, sleeping by day, and hunting deer and pigs by night. With their striped coats, they are almost impossible to see against a jungle background when they are standing still. Unlike most cats, tigers love bathing.

ZEBRA
Height: up to 1.6m

Zebras are stocky wild horses, with distinctive, black and white striped markings. There are 3 species, feeding on grass on the open plains or in lightly wooded areas in the east and south of the African continent. The zebra's stripes break up its outline very effectively, making it hard to spot against a background of sun-dappled, tall grass.

CHAMELEON
Length: 3.8–63.5cm

Chameleons are found in Africa, Arabia, and India. They can change colour in an instant, to blend in with their background, or when they are frightened. Each of their eyes can move independently, and they are capable of looking in any direction. Chameleons feed on insects, catching them on a sticky tongue, which they can shoot out further than the length of their own head and body combined!

MONARCH BUTTERFLY
Wingspan: up to 10cm
and VICEROY BUTTERFLY
Wingspan: up to 7.5cm

The Viceroy Butterfly is a perfect example of another form of disguise, called mimicry, where one animal mimics, or copies, the appearance of another. Birds eat butterflies, but avoid the Monarch because its blood tastes foul to them. The wing pattern of the Viceroy closely resembles the Monarch's wing pattern. So, although it would taste good to them, because it looks like a Monarch, birds leave the Viceroy Butterfly alone as well!

THE LARGEST ON LAND

Although the biggest of all the animals live in the sea (see page 24), there are some very large creatures on the land. Each of those shown below is unusual, not just in its size, but in some other way as well. The giraffe and the hippopotamus are found only in Africa. The elephant can be found in both Africa and Asia.

ELEPHANT
Height at shoulder: up to 4.2m

The two species, the African Elephant and the Indian Elephant, are highly intelligent vegetarians, the largest living land animals. The African Elephant is the larger, weighing up to 12 tonnes, and has bigger ears. An elephant's nose is extended to form a trunk, used for breathing, grasping things, drinking, and fighting. On each side of that are their tusks, enormous teeth, sometimes 3m long. Other teeth are also huge, some 10cm wide by 25cm long! For giant animals, elephants walk very softly, because their feet are padded.

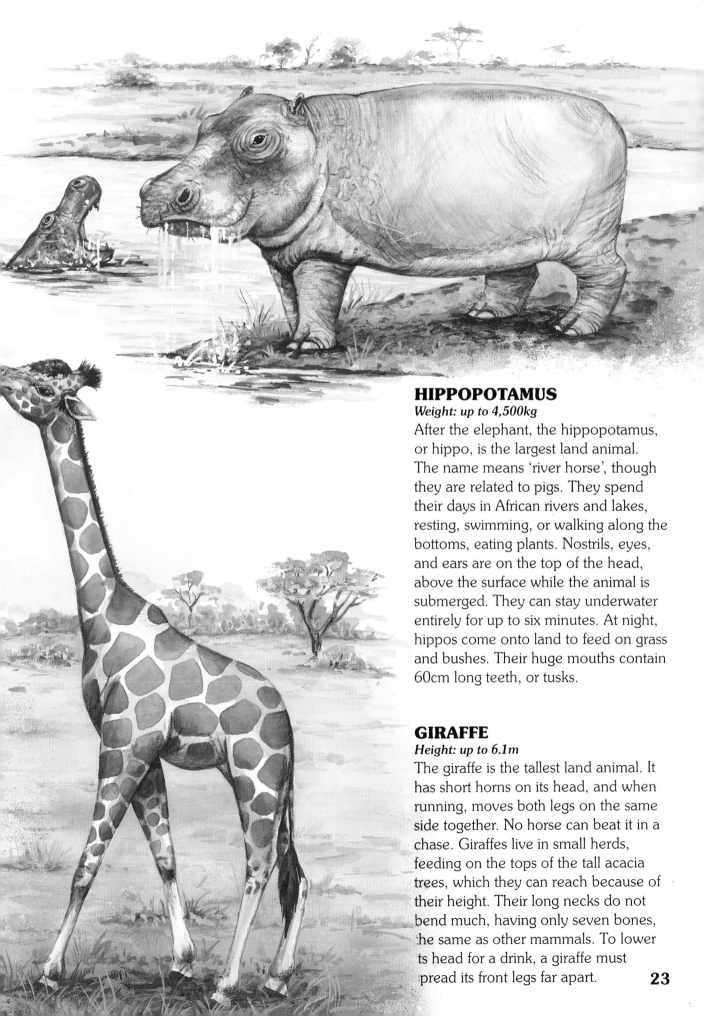

HIPPOPOTAMUS

Weight: up to 4,500kg

After the elephant, the hippopotamus, or hippo, is the largest land animal. The name means 'river horse', though they are related to pigs. They spend their days in African rivers and lakes, resting, swimming, or walking along the bottoms, eating plants. Nostrils, eyes, and ears are on the top of the head, above the surface while the animal is submerged. They can stay underwater entirely for up to six minutes. At night, hippos come onto land to feed on grass and bushes. Their huge mouths contain 60cm long teeth, or tusks.

GIRAFFE

Height: up to 6.1m

The giraffe is the tallest land animal. It has short horns on its head, and when running, moves both legs on the same side together. No horse can beat it in a chase. Giraffes live in small herds, feeding on the tops of the tall acacia trees, which they can reach because of their height. Their long necks do not bend much, having only seven bones, the same as other mammals. To lower its head for a drink, a giraffe must spread its front legs far apart.

GIANTS IN THE SEA

Some animals that live on the land can grow to a great size, but they are dwarfed by the creatures that live in the sea. Here are four marine giants. The largest of all, the Blue Whale, is a mammal.

MANTA RAY
Width: up to 7m
Manta Rays live on the ocean's surface, in warm waters. They eat tiny shellfish, using their 'horns', or head fins, to channel them into their broad mouths. Usually they are slow swimmers, but are capable of bursts of speed. Though they can weigh well over 1,300kg, a Manta Ray will sometimes leap right out of the water, apparently just for pleasure!

WHALE SHARK
Length: over 15m
Just like the Blue Whale, the Whale Shark, which is the largest fish in the world, is harmless to man, feeding mainly on plankton, a mixture of tiny shellfish and other organisms floating in the sea. It is an egg-laying fish, and specimens over 37cm long have been found in egg-cases. Whale Sharks are sluggish movers, living in all tropical waters.

BLUE WHALE
Length: up to 31m

The Blue Whale is the largest animal the world has ever known, but for all its size, this giant mammal nas no teeth. It feeds on tiny shellfish, weighing about 1g apiece, which it filters through the plates of baleen, or whalebone, in its mouth. During the Blue Whale's 120-day feeding season in the Antarctic, it will consume around 4 million shrimps each day! For the rest of the year, when they live in warmer waters, Blue Whales hardly eat at all!

GIANT SQUID
Length: up to 17.3m

The Giant Squid is a mollusc, a soft-bodied creature, like the oyster, a snail, or a slug. It is also a *cephalopod*, a word meaning 'head-foot'. Cephalopods are a species of mollusc in which the foot has been transformed into a set of tentacles armed with suckers, growing round the head. In the centre of its crown of tentacles, the squid has a mouth with a hard beak, with which it tears apart its prey. Giant Squids live in very deep water, and swim backwards, blowing water out of their body in a jet.

REMARKABLE INSECTS

Insects are very adaptable. Few of them live in the sea, but apart from that, they have conquered almost everywhere else. One kind of an insect or another will eat almost anything; from dung to solid wood to blood. Some of the more remarkable members of the insect family are shown here.

STICK-INSECT

Length: up to 33cm

The Giant Stick-Insect of Indonesia is the longest insect in the world. Stick-Insects look so much like twigs on the trees they live on that they are almost impossible to detect. They move and feed only by night, remaining motionless during the day. Few stick-insects are male, since the females lay fertile eggs without mating.

PRAYING MANTIS

Length: about 5cm

The name of this insect comes from its habit of holding its spiny forelegs folded like hands in prayer. A Praying Mantis will sit motionless in this position for long periods…until some unsuspecting victim comes close enough to be caught and devoured. They will even eat each other if they get the chance!

FIREFLY
Body Length: about 1cm

Fireflies are actually softwinged beetles, with light-producing organs on the body. At night, male fireflies fly about giving out a brilliant light, while the females sit in the grass responding with a fainter light. The light is cold, since the firefly can convert energy to light much more efficiently than our own electric light bulbs, for instance, which waste in the form of heat most of the energy needed to make them work.

BOMBARDIER BEETLE
Length: about 1cm

This beetle is a long-legged, fast-running hunter, one of a group known as ground beetles. The Bombardier Beetle gets its name from its defensive behaviour. When alarmed, it will fire out of its rear end, with a small bang, hot, corrosive liquid at an attacker!

CICADA
Body Length: about 3.5cm

A Cicada is a plant-feeding bug, with a long, piercing beak which is folded back under the head when not in use. The male Cicada is the loudest of all the insects, capable of producing a sound, by vibrating tiny membranes in the side of its body, which can be heard over 400m away.

FLIGHTLESS BIRDS

Most birds have breastbones that are shaped like the keel of a boat, and the birds' flying muscles are attached to this. Some birds, though, over a period of millions of years, have stopped using their wings, and their breastbones have flattened out and now look like rafts rather than keels. The Latin word for raft is *ratis*, so these birds are called ratite birds. Birds like penguins, though they do not fly, use their 'flying' muscles for swimming, so their breastbones are still shaped like keels, and they are not ratites. Ratites are the largest birds in the world.

OSTRICH
Height: up to 2.74m
The largest birds in the world live in the sandy wastes and on the thornbush-covered plains of Africa. There, they overlook every animal except the giraffe. They are also swift runners, capable of speeds of up to 64km/h. If cornered, an Ostrich will kick out with its powerful legs. Their claws are strong enough to damage a lion or a man. A fully-grown male Ostrich can weigh over 155kg, and an egg was once laid that weighed 2.3kg, big enough to provide about 20 people with a scrambled egg breakfast!

EMU
Height: about 1.8m

The Emu lives in Australia, and, after the ostrich, is the second-largest bird in the world. It is a nomadic, or wandering, species, and some individual Emus have been known to travel 1,000km in a year. These birds can cause considerable damage to crops, and in 1932 the state of Western Australia recruited the help of an army machine-gun unit to destroy them. But the birds scattered each time the soldiers opened fire, and the 'Emu War' was abandoned after a month.

CASSOWARY
Height: up to 1.6m

There are two species of Cassowary, both living in New Guinea, a large island to the north of Australia. They do not fly, and have blue and red skin on their heads and necks. Cassowaries also have a bony helmet, or casque, on the top of their head, which protects them as they race head-first through the undergrowth. The Dwarf Cassowary is regarded as the most dangerous bird in the world. Before nesting, the female will attack any creature nearby with its viciously-sharp, 10cm long claw.

KIWI
Height: up to 70cm

The thin, piping *kee-wee* cry of this bird echoing through the swampy forests of New Zealand is said to be the origin of its name. The largest Kiwi is about the size of a fat hen, and they are very difficult to see in the wild, being small, brown, and active only at night. Most birds have nostrils at the base of their bills, but, with Kiwis, the nostrils are at the very tip.

ANIMALS AT RISK

Man's actions are leading to the extinction of more and more species of animal life. Sometimes, animals are hunted until there are so few left alive that it is impossible for them to continue breeding. Sometimes, the destruction of the animals' natural surroundings for one reason or another causes an irreversible decline in the animal population. We are leaving fewer and fewer places where wild animals can live in peace. Sometimes, the cause of the destruction of wild life is the pollution that man spreads wherever he goes. By accident or intention, we poison other living creatures to death. Unless we are content to look forward to a future without wild animals, we must do all that we can now to stop this destruction. Shown here are just four of the many animals that are at risk.

YANGTZE RIVER DOLPHIN
Length: up to 2.4m

This shy, slim, long-beaked dolphin lives in China's greatest river, the Yangtze. Chinese legends say that it is the reincarnation of a drowned princess! Of all the dolphins, whales and porpoises, the Yangtze River Dolphin is the most endangered. Though now protected by law, some still die each year through being caught up in fishing gear. There are probably only about 300 of these mammals left alive in the wild.

GIANT PANDA
Length: up to 1.5m

A relative of the raccoons and bears the Giant Panda lives in the mounta of south-west China. It eats only bamboo, feeding for up to 16 hours day. Pandas must consume enormo amounts of bamboo in order to stay alive. But the bamboo forests are be cut down to make way for farms, an smaller and smaller wooded areas a left. As Pandas will not cross open country, an isolated animal cannot f itself a mate in another part of the remaining forest. Unfortunately, Gia Pandas do not breed well in captivit

OSPREY

Length: up to 60cm

The hawk-like Osprey lives entirely on fish which it catches in a spectacular way. The bird soars in circles above the water at heights of up to 60m. When it spots a target, it hovers momentarily, then plunges straight down, feet first, into the water, going right under the surface. After a few seconds, it re-merges with the fish clutched in its feet, which have spines on them to help them grip their slippery prey. Because the seas have become so polluted, the fish that the Ospreys eat are full of poison, and the numbers of these birds are now greatly reduced.

GORILLA

Height: up to 1.88m

Gorillas are man's closest animal relatives. They live in the rainforests of west and central Africa, eating plants and berries. There are two species, the Lowland Gorilla and the shaggier Mountain Gorilla. Because of the poverty and civil wars in the countries in which they live, their habitat is fast being destroyed. There are probably no more than 300 Mountain Gorillas left alive.

Index